Student:_____

Grade:_____

Our Year At A Glance

AUGUST

SEPTEMBER

OCTOBER

NOVEMBER

DECEMBER

JANUARY

GOAL	ACHIEVED
# of weeks_____	# of weeks_____
# of days _____	# of days _____

Our Year At A Glance

Important Dates

FEBRUARY
MARCH
APRIL
MAY
JUNE
JULY

GOAL	ACHIEVED
# of weeks_____	# of weeks _____
# of days _____	# of days _____

Yearly Subject Planner

Subject	Goal	Required Resource
Yoga		
Math		
Writing		
Reading		
Science		
Journal		
Music		
ART		

Curriculum Planner

Budget

Subject	Curriculum/Supplies	Cost
	Total	

Attendance Register

2020

Aug	Sep	Oct	Nov	Dec	Jan	Feb	Mar	Apr	May	June	July
								8			
								9			
								10			
								11			
								12			
								13			
								14			
								15			
								16			
								17			
								18			
								19			
								20			
								21			
								22			
								23			
								24			
								25			
								26			
								27			
								28			
								29			
								30			

Grade Register

Subject | |

Date	Assignment	Points Possible	Points Achieved	Grade

Grade Register

Subject [   ]

Date	Assignment	Points Possible	Points Achieved	Grade

Grade Register

Subject [ ]

Date	Assignment	Points Possible	Points Achieved	Grade

Grade Register

Subject [ ]

Date	Assignment	Points Possible	Points Achieved	Grade

Grade Register

Subject [   ]

Date	Assignment	Points Possible	Points Achieved	Grade

Grade Register

Subject [   ]

Date	Assignment	Points Possible	Points Achieved	Grade

Grade Register

Subject

Date	Assignment	Points Possible	Points Achieved	Grade

Grade Register

Subject

Date	Assignment	Points Possible	Points Achieved	Grade

Grade Register

Subject [ ]

Date	Assignment	Points Possible	Points Achieved	Grade

Grade Register

Subject

Date	Assignment	Points Possible	Points Achieved	Grade

Weekly Plan

Week Of MaR 30 – APR 3

To Do

1.

2.

3.

4.

5.

6.

7.

8.

9.

10.

Goals

Notes

Weekly Curriculum Plan

Week Of | MAR 30 - APR 3 |

Subject	Mon	Tues	Wed	Thur	Friday	☺
Yoga circle art	9-9³⁰ 9³⁰-945 945-10					😐 ☹

Subject	Mon	Tues	Wed	Thur	Friday	☺
Math	10-10³⁰					😐 ☹

Subject	Mon	Tues	Wed	Thur	Friday	☺
Writing	10³⁰-11					😐 ☹

Subject	Mon	Tues	Wed	Thur	Friday	☺
Reading	11-11³⁰					😐 ☹

Subject	Mon	Tues	Wed	Thur	Friday	☺
Science	1130-noon					😐 ☹

Lunch

Subject	Mon	Tues	Wed	Thur	Friday	☺
Journal	12³⁰-1					😐 ☹

Activity   1-2pm

Weekly Recap & Notes

Weekly Plan

Week Of [   ]

To Do

1.

2.

3.

4.

5.

6.

7.

8.

9.

10.

Goals

Notes

Weekly Curriculum Plan

Week Of

Subject	Mon	Tues	Wed	Thur	Friday	
						☺
						😐
						☹

Subject	Mon	Tues	Wed	Thur	Friday	
						☺
						😐
						☹

Subject	Mon	Tues	Wed	Thur	Friday	
						☺
						😐
						☹

Subject	Mon	Tues	Wed	Thur	Friday	
						☺
						😐
						☹

Subject	Mon	Tues	Wed	Thur	Friday	
						☺
						😐
						☹

Subject	Mon	Tues	Wed	Thur	Friday	
						☺
						😐
						☹

Weekly Recap & Notes

_____

_____

_____

_____

_____

_____

_____

_____

_____

_____

_____

_____

_____

Weekly Plan

Week Of [   ]

To Do

1.

2.

3.

4.

5.

6.

7.

8.

9.

10.

Goals

Notes

Weekly Curriculum Plan

Week Of

Subject	Mon	Tues	Wed	Thur	Friday	
						☺
						😐
						☹

Subject	Mon	Tues	Wed	Thur	Friday	
						☺
						😐
						☹

Subject	Mon	Tues	Wed	Thur	Friday	
						☺
						😐
						☹

Subject	Mon	Tues	Wed	Thur	Friday	
						☺
						😐
						☹

Subject	Mon	Tues	Wed	Thur	Friday	
						☺
						😐
						☹

Subject	Mon	Tues	Wed	Thur	Friday	
						☺
						😐
						☹

Weekly Recap & Notes

Weekly Plan

Week Of

To Do

1.

2.

3.

4.

5.

6.

7.

8.

9.

10.

Goals

Notes

Weekly Curriculum Plan

Week Of

Subject	Mon	Tues	Wed	Thur	Friday	
						☺ ☹

Subject	Mon	Tues	Wed	Thur	Friday	
						☺ ☹

Subject	Mon	Tues	Wed	Thur	Friday	
						☺ ☹

Subject	Mon	Tues	Wed	Thur	Friday	
						☺ ☹

Subject	Mon	Tues	Wed	Thur	Friday	
						☺ ☹

Subject	Mon	Tues	Wed	Thur	Friday	
						☺ ☹

Weekly Recap & Notes

Weekly Plan

Week Of

To Do

1.

2.

3.

4.

5.

6.

7.

8.

9.

10.

Goals

Notes

Weekly Curriculum Plan

Week Of

Subject	Mon	Tues	Wed	Thur	Friday	
						☺
						☺

Subject	Mon	Tues	Wed	Thur	Friday	
						☺
						☺

Subject	Mon	Tues	Wed	Thur	Friday	
						☺
						☺

Subject	Mon	Tues	Wed	Thur	Friday	
						☺
						☺

Subject	Mon	Tues	Wed	Thur	Friday	
						☺
						☺

Subject	Mon	Tues	Wed	Thur	Friday	
						☺
						☺

Weekly Recap & Notes

Weekly Plan

Week Of

To Do

1.

2.

3.

4.

5.

6.

7.

8.

9.

10.

Goals

Notes

Weekly Curriculum Plan

Week Of

Subject	Mon	Tues	Wed	Thur	Friday	
						☺
						😐
						☹

Subject	Mon	Tues	Wed	Thur	Friday	
						☺
						😐
						☹

Subject	Mon	Tues	Wed	Thur	Friday	
						☺
						😐
						☹

Subject	Mon	Tues	Wed	Thur	Friday	
						☺
						😐
						☹

Subject	Mon	Tues	Wed	Thur	Friday	
						☺
						😐
						☹

Subject	Mon	Tues	Wed	Thur	Friday	
						☺
						😐
						☹

Weekly Recap & Notes

Weekly Plan

Week Of

To Do

1.

2.

3.

4.

5.

6.

7.

8.

9.

10.

Goals

Notes

Weekly Curriculum Plan

Week Of

Subject	Mon	Tues	Wed	Thur	Friday	
						☺
						😐
						☹

Subject	Mon	Tues	Wed	Thur	Friday	
						☺
						😐
						☹

Subject	Mon	Tues	Wed	Thur	Friday	
						☺
						😐
						☹

Subject	Mon	Tues	Wed	Thur	Friday	
						☺
						😐
						☹

Subject	Mon	Tues	Wed	Thur	Friday	
						☺
						😐
						☹

Subject	Mon	Tues	Wed	Thur	Friday	
						☺
						😐
						☹

Weekly Recap & Notes

_____

_____

_____

_____

_____

_____

_____

_____

_____

_____

_____

_____

_____

Weekly Plan

Week Of

To Do

1.

2.

3.

4.

5.

6.

7.

8.

9.

10.

Goals

Notes

Weekly Curriculum Plan

Week Of

Subject	Mon	Tues	Wed	Thur	Friday

Subject	Mon	Tues	Wed	Thur	Friday

Subject	Mon	Tues	Wed	Thur	Friday

Subject	Mon	Tues	Wed	Thur	Friday

Subject	Mon	Tues	Wed	Thur	Friday

Subject	Mon	Tues	Wed	Thur	Friday

Weekly Recap & Notes

Weekly Plan

Week Of

To Do

1.

2.

3.

4.

5.

6.

7.

8.

9.

10.

Goals

Notes

Weekly Curriculum Plan

Week Of

Subject	Mon	Tues	Wed	Thur	Friday	☺ ☺ ☹

Subject	Mon	Tues	Wed	Thur	Friday	☺ ☺ ☹

Subject	Mon	Tues	Wed	Thur	Friday	☺ ☺ ☹

Subject	Mon	Tues	Wed	Thur	Friday	☺ ☺ ☹

Subject	Mon	Tues	Wed	Thur	Friday	☺ ☺ ☹

Subject	Mon	Tues	Wed	Thur	Friday	☺ ☺ ☹

Weekly Recap & Notes

Weekly Plan

Week Of

To Do

1.

2.

3.

4.

5.

6.

7.

8.

9.

10.

Goals

Notes

Weekly Curriculum Plan

Week Of

Subject	Mon	Tues	Wed	Thur	Friday	
						☺ ☹

Subject	Mon	Tues	Wed	Thur	Friday	
						☺ ☹

Subject	Mon	Tues	Wed	Thur	Friday	
						☺ ☹

Subject	Mon	Tues	Wed	Thur	Friday	
						☺ ☹

Subject	Mon	Tues	Wed	Thur	Friday	
						☺ ☹

Subject	Mon	Tues	Wed	Thur	Friday	
						☺ ☹

Weekly Recap & Notes

Weekly Plan

Week Of

To Do

1.

2.

3.

4.

5.

6.

7.

8.

9.

10.

Goals

Notes

Weekly Curriculum Plan

Week Of

Subject	Mon	Tues	Wed	Thur	Friday

Subject	Mon	Tues	Wed	Thur	Friday

Subject	Mon	Tues	Wed	Thur	Friday

Subject	Mon	Tues	Wed	Thur	Friday

Subject	Mon	Tues	Wed	Thur	Friday

Subject	Mon	Tues	Wed	Thur	Friday

Weekly Recap & Notes

Weekly Plan

Week Of

To Do

1.

2.

3.

4.

5.

6.

7.

8.

9.

10.

Goals

Notes

Weekly Curriculum Plan

Week Of

Subject	Mon	Tues	Wed	Thur	Friday	
						☺ ☐ ☹

Subject	Mon	Tues	Wed	Thur	Friday	
						☺ ☐ ☹

Subject	Mon	Tues	Wed	Thur	Friday	
						☺ ☐ ☹

Subject	Mon	Tues	Wed	Thur	Friday	
						☺ ☐ ☹

Subject	Mon	Tues	Wed	Thur	Friday	
						☺ ☐ ☹

Subject	Mon	Tues	Wed	Thur	Friday	
						☺ ☐ ☹

Weekly Recap & Notes

_____

_____

_____

_____

_____

_____

_____

_____

_____

_____

_____

_____

_____

Weekly Plan

Week Of

To Do

1.

2.

3.

4.

5.

6.

7.

8.

9.

10.

Goals

Notes

Weekly Curriculum Plan

Week Of

Subject	Mon	Tues	Wed	Thur	Friday

Subject	Mon	Tues	Wed	Thur	Friday

Subject	Mon	Tues	Wed	Thur	Friday

Subject	Mon	Tues	Wed	Thur	Friday

Subject	Mon	Tues	Wed	Thur	Friday

Subject	Mon	Tues	Wed	Thur	Friday

Weekly Recap & Notes

Weekly Plan

Week Of

To Do

1.

2.

3.

4.

5.

6.

7.

8.

9.

10.

Goals

Notes

Weekly Curriculum Plan

Week Of

Subject	Mon	Tues	Wed	Thur	Friday	
						☺ ☺ ☹

Subject	Mon	Tues	Wed	Thur	Friday	
						☺ ☺ ☹

Subject	Mon	Tues	Wed	Thur	Friday	
						☺ ☺ ☹

Subject	Mon	Tues	Wed	Thur	Friday	
						☺ ☺ ☹

Subject	Mon	Tues	Wed	Thur	Friday	
						☺ ☺ ☹

Subject	Mon	Tues	Wed	Thur	Friday	
						☺ ☺ ☹

Weekly Recap & Notes

Weekly Plan

Week Of

To Do

1.

2.

3.

4.

5.

6.

7.

8.

9.

10.

Goals

Notes

Weekly Curriculum Plan

Week Of

Subject	Mon	Tues	Wed	Thur	Friday	
						🙂 😐 ☹️

Subject	Mon	Tues	Wed	Thur	Friday	
						🙂 😐 ☹️

Subject	Mon	Tues	Wed	Thur	Friday	
						🙂 😐 ☹️

Subject	Mon	Tues	Wed	Thur	Friday	
						🙂 😐 ☹️

Subject	Mon	Tues	Wed	Thur	Friday	
						🙂 😐 ☹️

Subject	Mon	Tues	Wed	Thur	Friday	
						🙂 😐 ☹️

Weekly Recap & Notes

_____

_____

_____

_____

_____

_____

_____

_____

_____

_____

_____

_____

Weekly Plan

Week Of

To Do

1.

2.

3.

4.

5.

6.

7.

8.

9.

10.

Goals

Notes

Weekly Curriculum Plan

Week Of

Subject	Mon	Tues	Wed	Thur	Friday	
						☺ ☐ ☹

Subject	Mon	Tues	Wed	Thur	Friday	
						☺ ☐ ☹

Subject	Mon	Tues	Wed	Thur	Friday	
						☺ ☐ ☹

Subject	Mon	Tues	Wed	Thur	Friday	
						☺ ☐ ☹

Subject	Mon	Tues	Wed	Thur	Friday	
						☺ ☐ ☹

Subject	Mon	Tues	Wed	Thur	Friday	
						☺ ☐ ☹

Weekly Recap & Notes

_____

_____

_____

_____

_____

_____

_____

_____

_____

_____

_____

_____

Weekly Plan

Week Of

To Do

1.

2.

3.

4.

5.

6.

7.

8.

9.

10.

Goals

Notes

Weekly Curriculum Plan

Week Of

Subject	Mon	Tues	Wed	Thur	Friday	
						☺ ☹

Subject	Mon	Tues	Wed	Thur	Friday	
						☺ ☹

Subject	Mon	Tues	Wed	Thur	Friday	
						☺ ☹

Subject	Mon	Tues	Wed	Thur	Friday	
						☺ ☹

Subject	Mon	Tues	Wed	Thur	Friday	
						☺ ☹

Subject	Mon	Tues	Wed	Thur	Friday	
						☺ ☹

Weekly Recap & Notes

Weekly Plan

Week Of _____

To Do

1.

2.

3.

4.

5.

6.

7.

8.

9.

10.

Goals

Notes

Weekly Curriculum Plan

Week Of

Subject	Mon	Tues	Wed	Thur	Friday	

Subject	Mon	Tues	Wed	Thur	Friday	

Subject	Mon	Tues	Wed	Thur	Friday	

Subject	Mon	Tues	Wed	Thur	Friday	

Subject	Mon	Tues	Wed	Thur	Friday	

Subject	Mon	Tues	Wed	Thur	Friday	

Weekly Recap & Notes

Weekly Plan

Week Of

To Do

1.

2.

3.

4.

5.

6.

7.

8.

9.

10.

Goals

Notes

Weekly Curriculum Plan

Week Of

Subject	Mon	Tues	Wed	Thur	Friday	
						☺ ☐ ☹

Subject	Mon	Tues	Wed	Thur	Friday	
						☺ ☐ ☹

Subject	Mon	Tues	Wed	Thur	Friday	
						☺ ☐ ☹

Subject	Mon	Tues	Wed	Thur	Friday	
						☺ ☐ ☹

Subject	Mon	Tues	Wed	Thur	Friday	
						☺ ☐ ☹

Subject	Mon	Tues	Wed	Thur	Friday	
						☺ ☐ ☹

Weekly Recap & Notes

Weekly Plan

Week Of

To Do

1.

2.

3.

4.

5.

6.

7.

8.

9.

10.

Goals

Notes

Weekly Curriculum Plan

Week Of

Subject	Mon	Tues	Wed	Thur	Friday	
						☺ ☐ ☹

Subject	Mon	Tues	Wed	Thur	Friday	
						☺ ☐ ☹

Subject	Mon	Tues	Wed	Thur	Friday	
						☺ ☐ ☹

Subject	Mon	Tues	Wed	Thur	Friday	
						☺ ☐ ☹

Subject	Mon	Tues	Wed	Thur	Friday	
						☺ ☐ ☹

Subject	Mon	Tues	Wed	Thur	Friday	
						☺ ☐ ☹

Weekly Recap & Notes

_____

_____

_____

_____

_____

_____

_____

_____

_____

_____

_____

_____

Weekly Plan

Week Of

To Do

1.

2.

3.

4.

5.

6.

7.

8.

9.

10.

Goals

Notes

Weekly Curriculum Plan

Week Of

Subject	Mon	Tues	Wed	Thur	Friday	
						☺ ☺ ☹

Subject	Mon	Tues	Wed	Thur	Friday	
						☺ ☺ ☹

Subject	Mon	Tues	Wed	Thur	Friday	
						☺ ☺ ☹

Subject	Mon	Tues	Wed	Thur	Friday	
						☺ ☺ ☹

Subject	Mon	Tues	Wed	Thur	Friday	
						☺ ☺ ☹

Subject	Mon	Tues	Wed	Thur	Friday	
						☺ ☺ ☹

Weekly Recap & Notes

_____

_____

_____

_____

_____

_____

_____

_____

_____

_____

_____

_____

_____

Weekly Plan

Week Of

To Do

1.

2.

3.

4.

5.

6.

7.

8.

9.

10.

Goals

Notes

Weekly Curriculum Plan

Week Of

Subject	Mon	Tues	Wed	Thur	Friday	
						☺ ☺ ☹

Subject	Mon	Tues	Wed	Thur	Friday	
						☺ ☺ ☹

Subject	Mon	Tues	Wed	Thur	Friday	
						☺ ☺ ☹

Subject	Mon	Tues	Wed	Thur	Friday	
						☺ ☺ ☹

Subject	Mon	Tues	Wed	Thur	Friday	
						☺ ☺ ☹

Subject	Mon	Tues	Wed	Thur	Friday	
						☺ ☺ ☹

Weekly Recap & Notes

Weekly Plan

Week Of [   ]

To Do

1.

2.

3.

4.

5.

6.

7.

8.

9.

10.

Goals

Notes

Weekly Curriculum Plan

Week Of

Subject	Mon	Tues	Wed	Thur	Friday	
						☺ 😐 ☹

Subject	Mon	Tues	Wed	Thur	Friday	
						☺ 😐 ☹

Subject	Mon	Tues	Wed	Thur	Friday	
						☺ 😐 ☹

Subject	Mon	Tues	Wed	Thur	Friday	
						☺ 😐 ☹

Subject	Mon	Tues	Wed	Thur	Friday	
						☺ 😐 ☹

Subject	Mon	Tues	Wed	Thur	Friday	
						☺ 😐 ☹

Weekly Recap & Notes

Weekly Plan

Week Of [ ]

To Do

1.

2.

3.

4.

5.

6.

7.

8.

9.

10.

Goals

Notes

Weekly Curriculum Plan

Week Of

Subject	Mon	Tues	Wed	Thur	Friday	
						☺ ☻ ☹

Subject	Mon	Tues	Wed	Thur	Friday	
						☺ ☻ ☹

Subject	Mon	Tues	Wed	Thur	Friday	
						☺ ☻ ☹

Subject	Mon	Tues	Wed	Thur	Friday	
						☺ ☻ ☹

Subject	Mon	Tues	Wed	Thur	Friday	
						☺ ☻ ☹

Subject	Mon	Tues	Wed	Thur	Friday	
						☺ ☻ ☹

Weekly Recap & Notes

Weekly Plan

Week Of

To Do

1.

2.

3.

4.

5.

6.

7.

8.

9.

10.

Goals

Notes

Weekly Curriculum Plan

Week Of

Subject	Mon	Tues	Wed	Thur	Friday	
						☺ ☺ ☹

Subject	Mon	Tues	Wed	Thur	Friday	
						☺ ☺ ☹

Subject	Mon	Tues	Wed	Thur	Friday	
						☺ ☺ ☹

Subject	Mon	Tues	Wed	Thur	Friday	
						☺ ☺ ☹

Subject	Mon	Tues	Wed	Thur	Friday	
						☺ ☺ ☹

Subject	Mon	Tues	Wed	Thur	Friday	
						☺ ☺ ☹

Weekly Recap & Notes

Weekly Plan

Week Of

To Do

1.

2.

3.

4.

5.

6.

7.

8.

9.

10.

Goals

Notes

Weekly Curriculum Plan

Week Of _____

Subject	Mon	Tues	Wed	Thur	Friday	
						☺
						😐
						☹

Subject	Mon	Tues	Wed	Thur	Friday	
						☺
						😐
						☹

Subject	Mon	Tues	Wed	Thur	Friday	
						☺
						😐
						☹

Subject	Mon	Tues	Wed	Thur	Friday	
						☺
						😐
						☹

Subject	Mon	Tues	Wed	Thur	Friday	
						☺
						😐
						☹

Subject	Mon	Tues	Wed	Thur	Friday	
						☺
						😐
						☹

Weekly Recap & Notes

_____

_____

_____

_____

_____

_____

_____

_____

_____

_____

_____

_____

Weekly Plan

Week Of [   ]

To Do

1.

2.

3.

4.

5.

6.

7.

8.

9.

10.

Goals

Notes

Weekly Curriculum Plan

Week Of

Subject	Mon	Tues	Wed	Thur	Friday	
						☺ 😐 ☹

Subject	Mon	Tues	Wed	Thur	Friday	
						☺ 😐 ☹

Subject	Mon	Tues	Wed	Thur	Friday	
						☺ 😐 ☹

Subject	Mon	Tues	Wed	Thur	Friday	
						☺ 😐 ☹

Subject	Mon	Tues	Wed	Thur	Friday	
						☺ 😐 ☹

Subject	Mon	Tues	Wed	Thur	Friday	
						☺ 😐 ☹

Weekly Recap & Notes

_____

_____

_____

_____

_____

_____

_____

_____

_____

_____

_____

_____

Weekly Plan

Week Of

To Do

1.

2.

3.

4.

5.

6.

7.

8.

9.

10.

Goals

Notes

Weekly Curriculum Plan

Week Of

Subject	Mon	Tues	Wed	Thur	Friday

Subject	Mon	Tues	Wed	Thur	Friday

Subject	Mon	Tues	Wed	Thur	Friday

Subject	Mon	Tues	Wed	Thur	Friday

Subject	Mon	Tues	Wed	Thur	Friday

Subject	Mon	Tues	Wed	Thur	Friday

Weekly Recap & Notes

Weekly Plan

Week Of [ ]

To Do

1.

2.

3.

4.

5.

6.

7.

8.

9.

10.

Goals

Notes

Weekly Curriculum Plan

Week Of

Subject	Mon	Tues	Wed	Thur	Friday	
						☺ 😐 ☹

Subject	Mon	Tues	Wed	Thur	Friday	
						☺ 😐 ☹

Subject	Mon	Tues	Wed	Thur	Friday	
						☺ 😐 ☹

Subject	Mon	Tues	Wed	Thur	Friday	
						☺ 😐 ☹

Subject	Mon	Tues	Wed	Thur	Friday	
						☺ 😐 ☹

Subject	Mon	Tues	Wed	Thur	Friday	
						☺ 😐 ☹

Weekly Recap & Notes

_____

_____

_____

_____

_____

_____

_____

_____

_____

_____

_____

_____

Weekly Plan

Week Of

To Do

1.

2.

3.

4.

5.

6.

7.

8.

9.

10.

Goals

Notes

Weekly Curriculum Plan

Week Of

Subject	Mon	Tues	Wed	Thur	Friday	
						☺ ☹

Subject	Mon	Tues	Wed	Thur	Friday	
						☺ ☹

Subject	Mon	Tues	Wed	Thur	Friday	
						☺ ☹

Subject	Mon	Tues	Wed	Thur	Friday	
						☺ ☹

Subject	Mon	Tues	Wed	Thur	Friday	
						☺ ☹

Subject	Mon	Tues	Wed	Thur	Friday	
						☺ ☹

Weekly Recap & Notes

Weekly Plan

Week Of

To Do

1.

2.

3.

4.

5.

6.

7.

8.

9.

10.

Goals

Notes

Weekly Curriculum Plan

Week Of

Subject	Mon	Tues	Wed	Thur	Friday	
						☺ ☺ ☹

Subject	Mon	Tues	Wed	Thur	Friday	
						☺ ☺ ☹

Subject	Mon	Tues	Wed	Thur	Friday	
						☺ ☺ ☹

Subject	Mon	Tues	Wed	Thur	Friday	
						☺ ☺ ☹

Subject	Mon	Tues	Wed	Thur	Friday	
						☺ ☺ ☹

Subject	Mon	Tues	Wed	Thur	Friday	
						☺ ☺ ☹

Weekly Recap & Notes

Weekly Plan

Week Of

To Do

1.

2.

3.

4.

5.

6.

7.

8.

9.

10.

Goals

Notes

Weekly Curriculum Plan

Week Of

Subject	Mon	Tues	Wed	Thur	Friday	
						🙂 😐 🙁

Subject	Mon	Tues	Wed	Thur	Friday	
						🙂 😐 🙁

Subject	Mon	Tues	Wed	Thur	Friday	
						🙂 😐 🙁

Subject	Mon	Tues	Wed	Thur	Friday	
						🙂 😐 🙁

Subject	Mon	Tues	Wed	Thur	Friday	
						🙂 😐 🙁

Subject	Mon	Tues	Wed	Thur	Friday	
						🙂 😐 🙁

Weekly Recap & Notes

_____

_____

_____

_____

_____

_____

_____

_____

_____

_____

_____

_____

_____

Weekly Plan

Week Of

To Do

1.

2.

3.

4.

5.

6.

7.

8.

9.

10.

Goals

Notes

Weekly Curriculum Plan

Week Of

Subject	Mon	Tues	Wed	Thur	Friday	☺
						😐
						☹

Subject	Mon	Tues	Wed	Thur	Friday	☺
						😐
						☹

Subject	Mon	Tues	Wed	Thur	Friday	☺
						😐
						☹

Subject	Mon	Tues	Wed	Thur	Friday	☺
						😐
						☹

Subject	Mon	Tues	Wed	Thur	Friday	☺
						😐
						☹

Subject	Mon	Tues	Wed	Thur	Friday	☺
						😐
						☹

Weekly Recap & Notes

Weekly Plan

Week Of

To Do

1.

2.

3.

4.

5.

6.

7.

8.

9.

10.

Goals

Notes

Weekly Curriculum Plan

Week Of

Subject	Mon	Tues	Wed	Thur	Friday

Subject	Mon	Tues	Wed	Thur	Friday

Subject	Mon	Tues	Wed	Thur	Friday

Subject	Mon	Tues	Wed	Thur	Friday

Subject	Mon	Tues	Wed	Thur	Friday

Subject	Mon	Tues	Wed	Thur	Friday

Weekly Recap & Notes

_____

_____

_____

_____

_____

_____

_____

_____

_____

_____

_____

_____

_____

Weekly Plan

Week Of

To Do

1.

2.

3.

4.

5.

6.

7.

8.

9.

10.

Goals

Notes

Weekly Curriculum Plan

Week Of

Subject	Mon	Tues	Wed	Thur	Friday	
						☺
						😐
						☹

Subject	Mon	Tues	Wed	Thur	Friday	
						☺
						😐
						☹

Subject	Mon	Tues	Wed	Thur	Friday	
						☺
						😐
						☹

Subject	Mon	Tues	Wed	Thur	Friday	
						☺
						😐
						☹

Subject	Mon	Tues	Wed	Thur	Friday	
						☺
						😐
						☹

Subject	Mon	Tues	Wed	Thur	Friday	
						☺
						😐
						☹

Weekly Recap & Notes

Weekly Plan

Week Of

To Do

1.

2.

3.

4.

5.

6.

7.

8.

9.

10.

Goals

Notes

Weekly Curriculum Plan

Week Of

Subject	Mon	Tues	Wed	Thur	Friday	
						☺ ☻ ☹

Subject	Mon	Tues	Wed	Thur	Friday	
						☺ ☻ ☹

Subject	Mon	Tues	Wed	Thur	Friday	
						☺ ☻ ☹

Subject	Mon	Tues	Wed	Thur	Friday	
						☺ ☻ ☹

Subject	Mon	Tues	Wed	Thur	Friday	
						☺ ☻ ☹

Subject	Mon	Tues	Wed	Thur	Friday	
						☺ ☻ ☹

Weekly Recap & Notes

_____

_____

_____

_____

_____

_____

_____

_____

_____

_____

_____

_____

Weekly Plan

Week Of

To Do

1.

2.

3.

4.

5.

6.

7.

8.

9.

10.

Goals

Notes

Weekly Curriculum Plan

Week Of

Subject	Mon	Tues	Wed	Thur	Friday	
						☺ ☹

Subject	Mon	Tues	Wed	Thur	Friday	

Subject	Mon	Tues	Wed	Thur	Friday	

Subject	Mon	Tues	Wed	Thur	Friday	

Subject	Mon	Tues	Wed	Thur	Friday	

Subject	Mon	Tues	Wed	Thur	Friday	

Weekly Recap & Notes

Weekly Plan

Week Of [   ]

To Do

1.

2.

3.

4.

5.

6.

7.

8.

9.

10.

Goals

Notes

Weekly Curriculum Plan

Week Of

Subject	Mon	Tues	Wed	Thur	Friday

Subject	Mon	Tues	Wed	Thur	Friday

Subject	Mon	Tues	Wed	Thur	Friday

Subject	Mon	Tues	Wed	Thur	Friday

Subject	Mon	Tues	Wed	Thur	Friday

Subject	Mon	Tues	Wed	Thur	Friday

Weekly Recap & Notes

Weekly Plan

Week Of [   ]

To Do

1.

2.

3.

4.

5.

6.

7.

8.

9.

10.

Goals

Notes

Weekly Curriculum Plan

Week Of [   ]

Subject	Mon	Tues	Wed	Thur	Friday	
						☺ ☹

Subject	Mon	Tues	Wed	Thur	Friday	
						☺ ☹

Subject	Mon	Tues	Wed	Thur	Friday	
						☺ ☹

Subject	Mon	Tues	Wed	Thur	Friday	
						☺ ☹

Subject	Mon	Tues	Wed	Thur	Friday	
						☺ ☹

Subject	Mon	Tues	Wed	Thur	Friday	
						☺ ☹

Weekly Recap & Notes

_____

_____

_____

_____

_____

_____

_____

_____

_____

_____

_____

_____

Weekly Plan

Week Of

To Do

1.

2.

3.

4.

5.

6.

7.

8.

9.

10.

Goals

Notes

Weekly Curriculum Plan

Week Of

Subject	Mon	Tues	Wed	Thur	Friday	
						☺ 😐 ☹

Subject	Mon	Tues	Wed	Thur	Friday	
						☺ 😐 ☹

Subject	Mon	Tues	Wed	Thur	Friday	
						☺ 😐 ☹

Subject	Mon	Tues	Wed	Thur	Friday	
						☺ 😐 ☹

Subject	Mon	Tues	Wed	Thur	Friday	
						☺ 😐 ☹

Subject	Mon	Tues	Wed	Thur	Friday	
						☺ 😐 ☹

Weekly Recap & Notes

_____

_____

_____

_____

_____

_____

_____

_____

_____

_____

_____

_____

Ideas/Thoughts

Ideas/Thoughts

Ideas/Thoughts

Ideas/Thoughts

Ideas/Thoughts

Ideas/Thoughts

Ideas/Thoughts

Ideas/Thoughts

Ideas/Thoughts

Ideas/Thoughts

Ideas/Thoughts

Ideas/Thoughts

Ideas/Thoughts

Made in the USA
Middletown, DE
23 March 2020